The Bare Bones Dhammapada

Big Mind Big Love

by Tai Sheridan

The Bare Bones Dhammapada
Published by Create Space

© 2011 by Tai Sheridan

ISBN-13:
978-1461153771

ISBN-10:
1461153778

For electronic media, print,
and free download books by this author
please visit www.taisheridan.com

website: www.taisheridan.com
email: taisheridanzen@gmail.com

Dedication

To the essential goodness
of everyone

To be awake is to be alive

Henry David Thoreau

Contents

Introduction

The well loved *Dhammapada* is one of the oldest Buddhist texts on walking the path of enlightenment, love, integrity, and kindness. It contains four hundred twenty-three aphorisms attributed to Buddha, though they were likely compiled by many.

Even though the *Dhammapada* is a Buddhist classic of great beauty and wisdom, it is burdened by the stylistic and conceptual dust of the early and middle ages. I have wholly transformed the original by using contemporary and minimalistic images and have also renamed the sections in order to make them positive and meaningful for the modern reader.

The most profound changes resulted from stripping the *Dhammapada* of asceticism, monasticism, literalness, chauvinism, anachronisms, conceptualizations of evil, re-birth, gods, shame, and sensual denial. This rendition of the path of wisdom proffers universal truths for a contemporary audience regardless of gender, lifestyle or spiritual inclination.

I treasure the classic *Dhammapada*. This poetic version, while preserving the meaning, is not a substitute for the original; instead, it attempts to cut more directly and immediately to the chase of Buddha's wisdom. My hope is that *The Bare Bones Dhammapada* guides and encourages you, the reader, to live an authentic and kind life.

- Tai Sheridan, Kentfield, 2011

1 luminous being

1
everything luminous mind
ego invites anguish

2
everything luminous mind
calmly move with totality
color your shadow happy

3
resentment broils innards
shuts out blue green peace

4
drop vengeful mind
sip clear calm

5
hate gets you hated
kind gets you kinded

6
don't race from death
welcome short life
quell conflict
cool calm collected

7
passion habits torque
laziness a trap
you topple easy

8
rip pleasure out
of the driver's seat
mountains of faith
pizazz blows in

9
when ego habits drive
you can't hear real

10
practice be honest don't harm
truth opens big sky mind

11
hang ups on material
numbs spacious light being

12
real is real
garbage is garbage
ditch your ego
unity falls into place

13
lust leaks through mind holes
no practice no restraint

14
lust doesn't hang out
in calm mind

15
do bad anguish
do bad grieve

16
do good
dance joyfully

17
correct harms
offer continuous apology

18
do good throw a party
on the path sing and dance

19
wisdom sans integrity big foolishness
denial manipulation crowd pleasing big
foolishness

20
intellectual study not required
address ego passion aggression
happiness lives

2 alert joy

1
scatter brains walking dead
clear light mind vital

2
delicious attention
dancing with the awake

3
swim in oneness
awaken joyful harmony

4
integrity attention kindness truth
miracle of real you

5
an island of alertness
tactfulness equanimity
drowning in peace

6
stay alert
strike buddha gold

7
forget forgetfulness
side step sense indulgence
endless bliss waves

8
alertness a wide view
big love embraces all

9
gallop into now
leave dull mind in dust

10
hone your mind
ditch distractions

11
torch what binds you
revel in now

12
delighting in now
no going backwards

3 refined mind

1
stabilize monkey mind
the toughest task

2
as refined mind awakens
insane mind trembles

3
zig zag mind unreliable
stable mind happy

4
mind unknowable
watching it invites happy

5
watching wandering small mind
awakens big mind big heart

6
wishy washy attention
blocks wide open mind

7
sans passion ego
aggression duality
fear won't roost

8
fragile clay body
slice through duality
live wisely

9
you will die
everything humus

10
ill guided mind
harms you big

11
alert mind
your best friend

4 fragrant miracles

1
in death's domain
seek your miraculous lotus being

2
in death's domain
find your miraculous lotus being

3
body a mirage
romantic love foolish
go beyond habits

4
lost in pleasures
a flood of misery

5
lost in pleasures
living in harms way

6
sweetly meet people
a bee finding nectar

7
forget judging others
look in the mirror

8
flowery words garbage
if not living them

9
practice what you preach
lotus in full blossom

10
do a quintillion petals
worth of good

11
the perfume of your goodness
permeates the cosmos

12
the perfume of your integrity
jasmine essence

13
the perfume of your virtue
delightful infinite expansive

14

walk upright aware whole
nothing throws you off course

15 / 16

fragrant lilies grow in garbage
wise students grow amidst foolishness

5 foolish ways

1
long nights endless roads
foolish traveling sans truth light

2
don't hang with fools
choose light friends or solitude

3
money family no replacement
for true self big heart

4
studying foolishness
gets you wise

5
hanging with wise
doesn't guarantee wisdom

6
hanging with wise
invites big love big mind

7
no self love
big foolish crime

8
causing harm
endless grief

9
doing good
endless delight

10
sneaky manipulations
only foolish misery

11
foolishness wasted time
essential goodness the blessing

12
harming eventually
bursts into flames

13
fools arrogant with knowledge
lose essential goodness

14 / 15

seeking power praise corrupts spirit
looking down nose spoils essential goodness

16

chase fame gain
walk in peace
you choose

6 wise folks

1
stick with wise
invite feedback
breathe in support

2
deter foolish others
disregard what folks say

3
avoid harmful foolish folks
hang with wise kind folks

4
drink contentment joy
delight in truth

5
computer programers program
wise folks tame themselves

6
don't let praise blame run you
rest in mountain mind

7
rest in big calm
clear lake mind

8
grabbing lust thin air
balance happiness sorrow

9
material cravings manifest misery
just enough big integrity

10
hither thither yon folks chasing tails
big love big peace home sweet home

11
ditching ego the task
no self no birth no death

12
walk out of darkness
come home to homelessness
smile in solitude bliss

13
let it all go
settle into everything
as it is

14
want not
empty mind
joyful inter-being

7 awakened being

1
unbridled passion
won't touch you
when flying free

2
continual practice
letting everything go
home anywhere now

3
don't hang onto things
live balance
leave no traces
walk into emptiness

4
greed wrecks spiritual practice
muddy tracks everywhere you go

5

ditch ego pride
calm passions
maintain integrity
moon smiles on you

6

solid calm straight shooter
the misery stops here

7

calm mind calm activity calm speech
clear buddha stream runs this show

8

truthful sans passion surges
unbounded body flying free
wonderful noble you

9

each spot sacred
big mind blessing

10

forests of solitude
invite peaceful contemplation

8 one word

1
one wise word
annihilates a bunch of drivel

2
one wise verse
annihilates a thousand tomes

3
one truthful peace word
annihilates a thousand vacuous articulations

4
self possession
beats possessing others

5
wresting with your ego
beats controlling others

6
nobody can rob you
of calm big life

7
treasuring wise folks
beats tons of sacrifices

8
treasuring wise folks
beats tons of rituals

9
treasuring wise folks
beats tons of sacrifices and offerings

10
treasuring the elderly
uplifts life beauty joy energy

11
a day of honest contemplative living
beats ego's wanton ways

12
a day of honest contemplative living
beats a foolish unsettled life

13
a day of energetic focused living
beats a sleepy impoverished life

14
a day of clear insight and peace
beats a blind habitual mind

15
a day of transcendent being
beats a life mired in egoism

16
a day of big body big heart big mind
beats a lifetime of egoism

9 essential goodness

1
don't dilly dally
do good quit bad

2
fix mistakes quickly
repetition brings misery

3
repeat fine acts
essential goodness thrives

4
sometimes you get away with harm
trouble eventually catches up

5
harm awaits
around the corner
stick to goodness

6
don't be naïve
harming always a possibility
watch for small signs

7
trust patient practice
refinement arrives like rain

8
live well
by avoiding harm

9
essential goodness
wards off harm

10
offending innocent folk
always nasty blowback

11
goodness awakens liberation
harming awakens sorrow

12
nowhere to hide
from consequences

13
nowhere to hide
from death

10 no harm

1
death frightens
non harming the way
everybody one body

2
life so sweet
non harming the way
everybody one body

3
happiness impossible
if harming others

4
happiness possible
if not harming others

5
harsh words
boomerang back

6
welcome deep silence
one body peace
everything harmonious

7
living dying
torques everyone

8
ignoring harm done
a personal inferno

9
harming others
wracks up ten losses

10
harming others wracks up losses
screeching pain scads of losses busted bones

11
harming others wracks up losses
cross wired brains fingers pointing at you
loved ones dying poverty
property destroyed house on fire

12
harming others wracks up losses
hellish daily life

13
nothing saves you
from big spiritual doubts

14
anybody anywhere cultivating
calm mind steady practice
wholesome sex non harming
a living a buddha

15
rare people
practice tact

16
practice spiritual delights
vigor mindfulness truth seeking
kindness wisdom devotion
anguish slips away

17
chefs cook
wise people practice

11 creaky bones

1
no joy when hungers reign
walk out of shadows into light

2
dressing up illusory ego
won't end roller coaster passions
sickness hangs around
nothing to grab onto

3
fragile body
death awaits

4
this body
a sack of bones

5
temple of blood and bones
a full congregation of
disease death vanity deceit

6
body ages
timeless truth wise

7
without wisdom
you grow old
not wise

8
no awakening reality
sorrow upon sorrow

9
awakening big buddha body
hungers self die

10
no steady practice
begs lonely aging

11
no steady practice
sad regrets

12 loving myself

1
love yourself
watch yourself closely

2
daily goodness first
then guiding others

3
model goodness
minimize ego

4
you are your own wise teacher
quiet ego awaken peace

5
harming life
crushes you

6
you become
the harm you do

7

harming yourself easy
loving yourself harder

8

belittling wise folks
harms you

9

you create
goodness harm
who else?!

10

serve others
sans self neglect

13 living wise

1
help folks find
integrity vigor
truth acceptance

2
open big mind
follow truth path
big happiness

3
live ethically
big happiness

4
see world as mirage
transcend death

5
ah this beautiful world
fools drown in it
wise flow through it

6

waking from sleep
you illumine world

7

when your goodness thrives
you illumine world

8

blind people traipse through world
fly free see things as they are

9

liberate ego fly free
walk into marketplace

10

liars faithless unethical
harm at will

11

stingy foolish unhappy
giving the big happy

12

dharma path
beats owning
world universe

14 buddha being

1
all seeing
quelling passion
the unknown road

2
all seeing
sans hungers
the unknown road

3
silent indwelling
calm delightful restraint
buddhas hug you

4
incomprehensible human birth
incomprehensible suffering
incomprehensible dharma
buddhas rare birds

5
no bad deeds
doing good deeds
a clear mind
buddha being

6
harming uncool
toleration cool
big mind cool

7
no contempt no harm cool
restraint moderation cool
solitude kind thoughts cool
buddha school

8/9
passions never fill up
delight in unhooking

10
fearful folks
seek worldly refuge

11

no worldly safe harbor
from anguish

12
buddha dharma sangha
only safe harbor

13 / 14
noble truth suffering is
eight stone path suffering ends

15
awakened folks rare
everyone benefits

16
buddha blessed
dharma blessed
sangha blessed

17 / 18
honor all end hungers
sans sorrow fear
big benefit

15 big happy

1
in hating world
live lovingly

2
in sick world
live healthy

3
in pleasure world
live content

4
in materialistic world
live simply

5
in competitive world
live intrinsically

6
passions aggressions raging wildfires
body suffering certain
inner peace the blessing

7
greed bad habits reap sorrow
get it end it be peace

8
health contentment friendships finest gifts
ego detachment finest joy

9
calm solitude the nectar
anguish harming gone
joyous truth prevails

10
awakened friends yes!
continuous big love fest

11
foolish friends big unhappy
wise friends big happy

12
follow wise love folks
like moon follows stars

16 sweet contentment

1
violate your essential goodness
spiritual journey abandoned

2
painful disregarding tender
painful regarding distasteful
detach from pleasure pain

3
loss always hurts
cherish sans attachment
detached folks beyond pleasure pain

4
pleasure brings sorrow fear
non attachment awakens contentment

5
affection brings sorrow fear
non attachment awakens contentment

6
attachment brings sorrow fear
non attachment awakens contentment

7
desire brings sorrow fear
non attachment awakens contentment

8
craving brings sorrow fear
non attachment awakens contentment

9
people love virtuous
honest buddha folks

10
longing for miraculous reality
fuels your spiritual journey

11
long lost friends
welcome you
buddha coming home

12
live well
die well

17 rage not

1
ditch anger pride attachments
with nothing to grab - freedom!

2
quelling anger's march
big practice

3
love cooks anger
good cooks harm
giving cooks greed
truth cooks falsehood

4
speak real quell anger donate self
shimmering buddha light you

5
non harming settled body
just so peace

6
honed alertness truth study light seeking
drown out passion habits

7
whatever you do
some folks resentful

8
praise blame
passing winds

9 / 10
praise wise folks
spiritual maturity

11
stop wiggling about
settle down

12
stop uptight words
practice love words

13
calm monkey mind
refine head

14
restrain body speech mind
live centered presence

18 light barriers

1
are you spiritually
prepped for death's door?

2
a lamp unto yourself
wise kind awake

3
death arrives
sad you weren't ready

4
a lamp unto yourself
wisdom practice beyond birth death

5
work out habits
tad by tad

6
harming invites anguish

7
put your back
into spiritual path

8
immorality stinginess distorted intentions
blemish spirit endlessly

9
ignorance a grand pollution
may you fly free

10
egotists liars
the rude shameless
prideful polluted
lazy ignorant living

11
modest humble
searching detached kind
walking light path
arduous spiritual effort

12 / 13
killing lying stealing adultery addiction
grand self-destruction living deaths

14

ill intentioned folks sans restraint
avoid harm greed misery

15

envy wrecks calm mind

16

when envy ditched
peace reigns

17

passion aggression ego hungers
singe integrity

18

quit judging folks
gaze in mirror

19

fault finding stokes passions
no hunger appeasement here

20

nothing to hold onto
quit grabbing air

21
nothing to hold onto
stabilize emptiness

19 non harming

1
force destroys solutions
listening opens viewpoints

2
non-violence illumines
wisdom justice

3
wise folks live calm
sans fear hate

4
watering dharma practice
the essential life

5
age alone
won't make wise

6
wise elders manifest
truth non harming
moderation restraint

7

looking good
fancy words
ego envy slick
wisdom path not

8

sans envy aggression ego
wise respectful indeed

9

self image won't abate
rampant passion greed

10

spiritual students
quell habits

11

don't confuse outer support
with inner worth

12

awake good
beyond fame blame
real buddha now

13/14

quiet won't wise up fools
a sage essential goodness
seeing things as is

15

all harming ignoble
non-violence noble

16/17

detachment from desire
true freedom

20 light road

1
four nobles finest
eight stones finest
detachment finest
clear seeing finest

2
clear path
clear insight
contented being
take this road

3
end suffering
yes!

4
only you awaken you
end habits find luminosity

5
all things pass
wake up!

6
sorrow abounds
find big happy!

7
all things insubstantial
find big real!

8
laziness bedevils enlightenment

9
stay alert talk kind act kind
the integrity road

10
devotion brings wisdom
follow true heart

11
discard whole passion deck
ditch fear fly free

12
lust trashes peace mind

13
gently destroy illusory ego
no self ever was

14
no better circumstances
than what you got now

15
death seeks out
distractions attachment

16
nobody cancels
death's invitation

17
know death is coming
practice vigorously fly free

21 wise bits

1
drop small tinglings
for big bliss

2
hating others
zeroes out happiness

3
neglecting tasks harms
arrogant passions unbridle

4
alertness doing good restraining harm
arrogant passions quelled

5
sans cravings ego attachments
contentment reigns

6
sans lust laziness
angst doubt hate
contentment reigns

7

buddha students
awaken sky mind
moment by moment
in light

8

buddha students
awaken sky mind
moment by moment
in truth

9

buddha students
awaken sky mind
moment by moment
in community

10

buddha students
awaken sky mind
moment by moment
in ceaseless body aging

11
buddha students
awaken sky mind
moment by moment
in non harming

12
buddha students
awaken sky mind
moment by moment
in contemplation

13
life difficulties always abound
unhook sorrows fly free

14
virtue devotion
world blessed

15
harmful folks dark shadows
good folks light beacons

16
enjoy solitudes
enjoy quelling passions

22 clear intentions

1
lying invites anguish

2
even spiritual
seekers teachers
can cause harm

3
don't use others
when out of sorts

4
sexual insanity
wrecks havoc

5
sexual acting out
brings fear ridicule

6
self-denial harms

7
half hearted practice
wastes time

8
act with total commitment

9
harming torments
kindness settles

10
ever vigilant
avoids anguish

11
self-blame harmful
lacking contrition harmful

12
inappropriate fear distressful
no appropriate fear distressful

13
seeing mistakes when none problematic
not seeing mistakes when real problematic

14

clear eyes see
mistakes as mistakes
truth as truth

23 steady virtue

1
when slammed
turn the other cheek

2
tolerance
the noble bearing

3
best when you
are passions boss

4
refinement presence peace
awaken emptiness

5
rampant mind
difficult to settle

6
indolence greed flip-flopping about
stuck in earthly mud

7

tame monkey mind
each moment

8

watch yourself closely
run from loathsomeness

9

stick with wise friends
joyfully climb spirit mountain

10

if no wise friends
solitude next best

11

solitude and kindness
better than immature friends

12

good friends good works
refined contentment
big happy

13
serving parents bliss
serving disenfranchised bliss
serving buddhas bliss

14
steady virtue bliss
steady faith bliss
steady wisdom bliss
steady goodness bliss

24 untamed hungers

1
cravings geometric
monkey mind cycles

2
dark cravings
feed sorrows

3
settling passions
awakens contentment

4
bless your effort
moderating passions

5
passions invite
repeated anguish

6
passion surges
drown you

7
wisdom slices
through passion

8
passion addiction
destroys transcendence

9
addiction cycles endless
big ego trap

10
hunger cycles endless
freedom flies beyond

11
backsliding passion easy
watch out!

12
attaching to people things
hinders happy inter-being

13
strong practice
walks away
from attachments

14

lust fires a spider web
wisdoms avoids being caught

15

beyond past present future
loathsome thoughts grow hungers
let go fly free

16

worldly mind treats arouse passions
hungers on the rise

17

settle mind
contemplate anguish
slice through attachments

18

fearless and content
big body big heart big mind

19

ending passions attachments
the sage within

20
big body big love big mind
you your own teacher now

21
truth the big gift
equanimity the king queen

22
materialism wipes out integrity

23
passion blights
love fields

24
non harming
fruitful benefit

25
making offerings
to kind folks
fruitful benefit

26
make offerings
to contented folks
fruitful benefit

25 settled way

1

moderating senses
a very good thing

2

moderating body speech mind
shackles drop away
freedom awakens

3

students of the way
practice grounded presence
delightful meditation

4

conquer ego
awaken light
sweet words

5

students swimming in truth
don't look back

6

envy destroys calm
big gratitude quells it

7

gratitude knows no bounds
opens vigorous living

8

fly free of mind body
dwell happy beyond sorrows

9

compassionate living
awakens big happy
unconditioned wonder

10

ditch ego passion aggression
resplendent clear light

11

work with your life until
flying free in empty sky

12

meditation focuses mind
awakens contentment

13
wisdom concentration
big emptiness the open door

14
self contented
calm heart mind
clear eyes yes!

15
watching things come go
wisdom bliss nectar

16
fine friends moderate senses
calm mind easy restraint
living buddha!

17
welcome all live integrity
big joy ends anguish

18
shed passions aggressions
dead ego petals

19
calm body speech mind
real deal buddha

20
big self encourages little self
happiness thrives

21
big self protects vulnerability
big self your destiny
settle yourself down

22
fill with spirit delights
fill with faith in buddha you
unconditioned peace arising now

23
dharma students illumine world
moon from behind clouds

26 buddha you

1
stop hungers practice sincerely
welcome uncreated realize no self

2
other shore awakens
calm insightful
nothing binds

3
detached from sense
fearless free
buddha everywhere you

4
contemplative sans passion
stable good awake
buddha everywhere you

5
radiant buddha wisdom
lights day night

6

essential goodness
balanced views clean living
buddha everywhere you

7

don't slight buddhas
don't react to slights

8

let go pleasure attachments
let go harmful thoughts
suffering wanes

9

maintain non harming
body speech mind
buddha everywhere you

10

honor all buddhas
with big heart big mind

11

truth not inherited
truth integrity awakened

12
outwardly good-looking
inwardly obsessed
passion jungle

13
humble simple contemplative
buddha everywhere you

14
free from passion
materialism attachments
buddha everywhere you

15
fearless detached
gone beyond
buddha everywhere you

16
beyond aggression passions
beyond conditioned habits
beyond duality
buddha everywhere you

17
patiently endure harm
buddha everywhere you

18
sans aggression guile
practicing vigorously
kind present restrained
buddha everywhere you

19
detached from pleasure
buddha everywhere you

20
sans anguish attachments
not identified with body
buddha everywhere you

21
vast wisdom clear mind
essential goodness prevailing
one big body
buddha everywhere you

22
open to all
living simply
buddha everywhere you

23
stopping harm
buddha everywhere you

24
calm tolerant unattached
buddha everywhere you

25
sans lust hate pride doublespeak
buddha everywhere you

26
gentle talk truth words
buddha everywhere you

27
stealing naught
buddha everywhere you

28
sans hungers passions habits
buddha everywhere you

29
sans hunger doubts
awakened inter-being
no birth no death
buddha everywhere you

30
no attainment
happy free
buddha everywhere you

31
clear moon mind
essentially good serene
beyond living dying
buddha everywhere you

32
through the open door
sans self hungers doubts attachments
contemplative calm
buddha everywhere you

33
detached pleasure ditched hungers
a floating cloud everywhere home
buddha everywhere you

34
detached pleasures ditched thirsts
a floating cloud
beyond living dying
buddha everywhere you

35
beyond folks
beyond buddhas
beyond awakening
beyond attachments
buddha everywhere you

36
beyond pleasure pain
beyond passion
beyond body identity
buddha everywhere you

37
seeing arising mind
detached from things
content within
one light body
buddha everywhere you

38
continual not knowing
detached senses
buddha everywhere you

39
not mired in past present future
commingled with things
detached from things
buddha everywhere you

40
fearless spiritual warrior
free from passions bad habits
buddha everywhere you

41
all seeing eye
no body no mind
luminous wisdom
buddha everywhere you

About the Author

Poet Tai Sheridan is a Zen priest in the Shunryu Suzuki lineage. He trained with San Francisco Zen Center, Dharma Eye Zen Center, Berkeley Zen Center, Zen Heart Sangha, and The Shogaku Zen Institute. He specializes in transforming ancient Buddhist and Zen texts into accessible and inspirational verses.

For other books by this author
please visit www.taisheridan.com

You can contact Tai Sheridan at
taisheridanzen@gmail.com

Printed in Great Britain
by Amazon